Libby the Loving and Kind

Cares for the Earth

JLH Tavares

Libby the Loving and Kind

Cares for the Earth

JLH Tavares

ISBN: 978-1-7368024-5-8 (Hardback)
ISBN: 978-1-7368024-4-1 (Paperback)
ISBN: 978-1-7368024-3-4 (Digital Online)

Library of Congress Control Number: 2022909450

Any references to historical events, real people, or real places are used fictitiously- Names, characters, and places are products of the author's imagination.

Our books may be purchased in bulk for promotional, educational, or business use. Please contact your local bookseller or the Maor Media Sales Department at maormediaglobal@gmail.com
First printing edition 2022.

Maor Media
1317 Edgewater Drive
Suite 3774
Orlando, Florida 32804

20 minutes a day can open a universe of opportunities.

This book is dedicated to the children all over the world
that will care for, love, nurture, and protect the
Earth: our common ground.

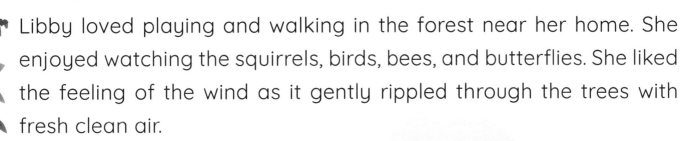

Libby loved playing and walking in the forest near her home. She enjoyed watching the squirrels, birds, bees, and butterflies. She liked the feeling of the wind as it gently rippled through the trees with fresh clean air.

However, one early morning Libby noticed something different on the horizon where there had always been a forest.

They were tearing down the trees!
Libby took a deep breath in and worriedly asked,
"What's happening with the forest?"

Farmer Martin replied, "There are more people in the world, and with more people, it also means they need places to live, forest resources, and food to eat. So, they can either expand or go higher. Unfortunately, you can see for yourself that some forest space must be sacrificed for homes, food, and resources."

Libby was distraught. Soon, there would no longer be a forest!

She would no longer be able to watch the morning sun fill the forest with its beautiful golden light or watch the animals as they went about their day.

As the forest continued to shrink, Libby became more unhappy. She felt helpless as she watched the forest she loved so dearly disappear.

She tried many of the special coping skills she learned that would normally pick up her spirit and make her happier.

Deep breaths. Check.

Long walks with her friends and animals. Check.

Listening to music and dancing. Check.

However, Libby was still unhappy. She sat down and allowed herself to feel her emotions, and as she cried, she thought to herself, "What is making me so sad?"

She reflected and thought deeply about all the changes that were happening and realized what was making her so sad.

She recognized the world was changing.
The forest she loved was shrinking.
But what could she do?

On her way to school the next morning, Libby asked Farmer Martin, "What will happen to the animals that live in the forest?"

"What will happen to the trees they took away?"

"What can we do about the forest going away?"

Farmer Martin kindly said, "Well, Libby, the forest may not come back, if we do nothing. People need places to live, food to eat, and wood to build their houses.

We need land to grow food too. The best action we can take now is to figure out how we can make a positive change, even when we see our surroundings change in ways we don't agree with or like.

When we see a problem, we can do our best to look at those challenges in order to find a solution to solve the problem, together.

The solution starts with us. The small acts we do ourselves can make a big difference in our world."

Farmer Martin asked Libby, "What would you like to do to make a positive change?"

Libby thought deeply about her answer as she went to school.

At school, Libby talked to her friends, Grace, Liz, Lawson, and Eli about what was happening with the forest. She shared what she had learned, and they wanted to know more about what they could do.

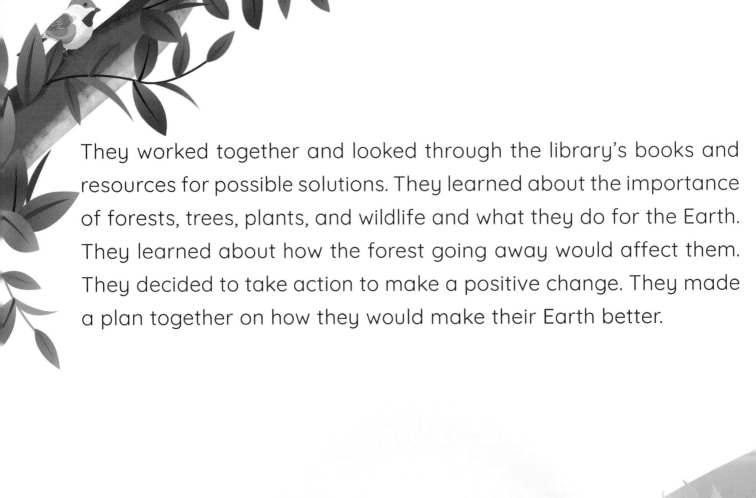

They worked together and looked through the library's books and resources for possible solutions. They learned about the importance of forests, trees, plants, and wildlife and what they do for the Earth. They learned about how the forest going away would affect them. They decided to take action to make a positive change. They made a plan together on how they would make their Earth better.

They were all very excited about their new project and how each would act to do something different but meaningful to care for their common ground.

Libby and Farmer Martin made a special day to plant the acorns and pine cones they gathered from their forest nearby. He said, "Let's plant these seeds for the future. Remember, the day you plant the seed is not the same day you harvest its fruits."

They also went to their local garden center to buy garden supplies, trees, flowers, flower seeds, a birdhouse, and a bag of seeds for the birds and squirrels.

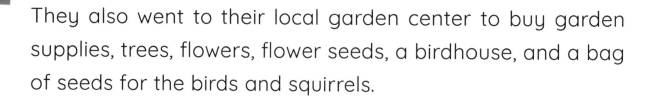

As Farmer Martin and Libby planted the trees, he explained, "When we plant a variety of trees to replace the ones the forest lost, we help to give animals shelter and shade from the hot sun. We also enhance the effective growth of fruits, seeds, and nuts for food. These trees create oxygen for us to breathe, they clean the air, hold the soil in place, and break the winds that sometimes cause erosion.

There is so much we can do to make the world a better place to live. We can also allow others to share the beauty and freedom of growing and enjoying the Earth, while maintaining proper boundaries. It's about a balance or middle ground where we do our best to have harmony between nature and people."

As she planted each tree, she sang a little song to help them grow.

They planted a variety of plants. The flowers had wonderful smells to attract and feed the bees, butterflies, birds, insects, and other pollinators. As Farmer Martin and Libby planted the flowers and plants, he explained, "When we grow plants in place of the ones the forest lost, we can help the Earth with these plants that produce oxygen and food for people, animals, and insects to eat."

She planted seeds in pots to share
with her friends that lived in the city.

As she planted the flowers, she whispered
an encouraging word to help them grow.

Libby put up a birdhouse and bird feeder filled with seeds and nuts that would be helpful for the squirrels and birds.

Libby was excited to share all she had done with her friends and see their solutions and ideas come to life.

Liz shared how she planted a garden with flowers and vegetables.

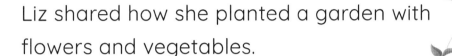

Grace shared how she planted trees to help produce oxygen, clean the air, and provide shelter and shade.

Lawson shared how he and his parents were caring for bees and building beehives.

Eli and his family improved the forest. They removed litter and recycled them so that the animals and the waterways would be free of pollutants and debris.

Libby looked at all the wonderful ways she and her friends were able to help the Earth, the forest, and the animals. She realized that despite how small she and her friends were, they could care for the Earth by planting trees and flowers, recycling, tending a garden, cleaning the forest, and picking up litter. Each act of kindness counts.

Later, she looked over the land filled with happy faces, beautiful gardens, new trees, and nature preserve. She was grateful for the Earth around her, and a warm glow began to radiate from within and formed a beautiful smile of joy upon her face.

Discussion and Action

Why is it important to care for the Earth and environment?

What are some ways you would like to make a positive impact on the Earth?

Discuss how you can do your part.

Look at some fun ideas to get involved to make the world a better place to live.

Let's get thinking!

Reuse and Recycle

Mindful water and energy use

Plant a tree

Plant a garden

Pick up litter

Put up a bird feeder or birdhouse

About the Author

JLH Tavares holds a Bachelor of Science in Psychology and a
Master of Social Work from the University of Southern California.
She is an author, entrepreneur, world traveler, and U.S. Army veteran
who lives on the eastern shore of Florida with her family.
She hopes her words will enrich and empower children, strengthen
their resilience, and encourage loving kindness in the world.

We hope you enjoyed the book.
Your opinion matters. Please leave a review.
Tell others why you enjoyed this book. Thank you.

Printed by Amazon Italia Logistica S.r.l.
Torrazza Piemonte (TO), Italy

60555481R00025